Lean Startup

The Complete Step-by-Step Lean Six Sigma Startup Guide

Jeffrey Ries

© **Copyright 2018 by Jeffrey Ries. All rights reserved.**

This document is geared towards providing exact and reliable information regarding topic and issue covered. The publication is sold with the idea that the publisher is not required to render accounting, officially permitted, or otherwise, qualified services. If advice is necessary, legal or professional, a practiced individual in the profession should be ordered.

From a Declaration of Principles which was accepted and approved equally by a Committee of the American Bar Association and a Committee of Publishers and Associations.

In no way is it legal to reproduce, duplicate, or transmit any part of this document in either electronic means or in printed format. Recording of this publication is strictly prohibited and any storage of this document is not allowed unless with written permission from the publisher. All rights reserved.

The information provided herein is stated to be truthful and consistent, in that any liability, in terms of inattention or otherwise, by any usage or abuse of any policies, processes, or directions contained within is the solitary and utter responsibility of the recipient reader. Under no circumstances will any legal responsibility or blame be held against the publisher for any reparation, damages, or monetary loss due to the information herein, either directly or indirectly.

Respective authors own all copyrights not held by the publisher.
The information herein is offered for informational purposes solely, and is universal as so. The presentation of the information is without contract or any type of guarantee assurance.

The trademarks that are used are without any consent, and the publication of the trademark is without permission or backing by the trademark owner. All trademarks and brands within this book are for clarifying purposes only and are the owned by the owners themselves, not affiliated with this document.

Table of Contents

Introduction 4

Chapter 1: Lean Startup Options 9

Chapter 2: Create a Useful Lean Startup Experiment...............21

Chapter 3: Growing a Startup..28

Chapter 4: Six Sigma Basics 40

Chapter 5: Implementing Six Sigma 47

Chapter 6: Additional Strategies 54

Conclusion 63

Introduction

Congratulations on getting a copy of *Lean Startup: The Complete Step-by-Step Lean Six Sigma Startup Guide* and thank you for doing so. There are two questions that any company can ask to both reduce unnecessary failure while at the same time ensuring that the company focuses only on ideas that have promising potential. They are:

- Should we build this new service or product?
- How can we improve our odds of success with this new thing?

The Lean method is equally useful for startup companies as it is for Fortune 500 companies. It may have its roots in the technology sector but it is already being used in virtually every industry across the board. While there is lots of confusion around it, the Lean Startup system can help companies of all sizes in a lot of different ways.

While the term "startup" generally has very specific connotations in the business world, in this instance, "startup" simply means any team that is planning to create a new product or service whose future isn't 100 percent certain yet. Generally speaking, it makes far more sense to classify startups as enterprises taking on the challenge amidst uncertainty, than by categories like market sector, size or even age of the company.

With this definition in mind, you will find that there are a few main areas in which a startup faces the greatest amount of uncertainty, otherwise known as risk. Technical or product risk can be summed up by the question "Can it be built?" As an example, doctors who are currently working towards a cure for cancer can be thought of as a startup institution because there is a very large technical risk and this area of study has been going on for quite some time with no hint of success. However, if they do discover a cure, there is absolutely no market risk because its target market would definitely buy it.

Market risk, also known as customer risk, is simply the risk when the product or service reaches the market and no one is actually going to want to buy it. A cautionary example of this type of risk is a company named Webvan that spent millions and millions of dollars creating an automated means of buying groceries online. The only problem is that they tried to get this system up and running in the early 2000s. This is a time when many people were still getting comfortable with the concept of the internet in general but the comfort in buying everyday products online did not follow until nearly a decade.

The business model risk is the risk associated with taking a good idea and building a functioning business plan around it. Even if you already have a good idea, the right business model could very well not be visible until the service is up and running. As an example, when Google started its original business plan of selling advertisements based on previous searches, the plan wasn't clear because no one had done that sort of thing before.

While every company will need to deal with these risks to varying degrees, the biggest risk that most new products or services struggle with is customer risk. It can be difficult to determine the value of something new for customers who haven't experienced it yet. The tricky part here is that in most instances, it will actually appear that the product risk is the most urgent risk. After all, most new ideas don't make it this far without an assumption that someone, somewhere is going to want the product or service at hand. This assumption, then, can lead to a much costlier course of action wherein you do the work to create the product or service before offering it to anyone.

This is where the Lean Startup system comes into play. This technology potentially stops you from being one of the millions of companies out there that has a good idea and a cool product but had crashed and burned because they inherently relied on assumptions about consumer behavior that simply turned out not be true. It is important to think in terms of risk as opposed to company history because in doing so, you will find that many large companies have startup organizations within them. As an example, consider the Gillette razor company who felt that there was little risk in adding the fifth blade to their flagship line of razors because they knew the business model, the market, and the product ins and outs. However, the company that owns Gillette, Proctor and Gamble, operates a startup in the form of its research and development division that focuses specifically on hair removal. With each new idea, this division seems like a startup because they have no known variable which means everything they are working on is extremely risky.

Currently, one of the well-known companies that using the Lean Startup system is General Electric, which is also one of the largest companies in the world. The company has trained more than 10,000 managers around the world to use Lean Startup principles and has used the system to successfully improve the end result on all of their products including refrigerators and diesel engines.

To follow in their footsteps, the following chapters will discuss how to operate a Lean Startup successfully, starting with an overview of the Lean Startup methodology. Next, you will learn how to create a trial startup system that is not only useful but also designed to provide you with as much viable information as possible. You will then learn how to take a successful startup and grow it until it reaches its full potential. From there you will learn about adding Six Sigma and other Lean tools to your startup for maximum efficacy.

There are plenty of books on this subject on the market, thanks again for choosing this one! Every effort was made to ensure it is full of as much useful information as possible, please enjoy!

Chapter 1: Lean Startup Options

While the idea of the Lean Startup has been around since 2011, many companies are still coming to grips with everything the system has to offer. This is despite the fact that most of the ideas presented in this system were hardly new. This is largely due to the fact that the system actually offers more value to established organizations than it does to startups. However, startups can still be able to build a Lean system from the ground up if they choose to.

Lean Startup methodology

Build, measure, and learn: Perhaps more than anything else in recent history, the application of the scientific method to demolish uncertainty, where innovation is concerned, has transformed the way breakthroughs happen. Broken down, this includes the process of defining a hypothesis, creating a prototype to test the hypothesis, testing the prototype (and thus the hypothesis) and then adjusting as needed. While this may seem simple, it has the potential to generate massive results by enabling companies to take risks on smaller ideas without breaking the bank in the process.

The build, measure, and learn approach can be used for virtually everything, not just entirely new ideas. It can be used to test things like customer service ideas, the process of managerial review, or even a new feature for an existing product or service. As long as you can perform a test that clearly validates or disproves the initial hypothesis, then you will be good to go because you must be able to gather enough data to justify approving or vetoing the idea.

The goal, then, is to do everything possible in order to ensure that build, measure, and learn process proceeds from start to finish as quickly as possible. This will make it feasible to run the process multiple times if needed, while also making it clear when such additional runs are needed. As such, it is important to have a very specific idea for each test because as more variables are added, the more difficult it will be to determine results with any real degree of accuracy. When it comes to products and services, this means determining if they are either wanted or needed by the target audience.

Minimal viable product: Generally speaking, most product development involves an extreme amount of work up front. The process involves working through the full specifications of the product, as well as a significant initial investment when it comes to capital in order to build and test multiple iterations of the product. The Lean Startup process thus encourages building only enough of the product in question to make it through a single round of the build, measure, and learn process at a time. This is what is known as the minimal variable product.

The minimal variation of the product is what enables a full cycle of the build, measure, and learn loop to be completed with the least amount of required time and effort on the part of the team. This may not be something as simple as writing a new line of code, it could be an elaborate process that outlines the customer journey, or a complete set of mockups made out of a cheaper substitute. As long as it is enough to test the hypothesis, then it is good to go.

Validated Learning: An important part of the Lean Startup process is ensuring that you are testing your hypothesis with an eye towards the right metrics. Failing to do so can make it easy to focus on vanity metrics instead. Focusing on vanity metrics may make you feel as though you are making progress while not actually telling you all that much about the value of the product. For example, for Facebook, the vanity metrics are the things like the total number of "Likes" that have been received or the number of total accounts created. The real meat and potatoes are in metrics such as the amount of time the average user spends on the service per week. Early on, the metric that validated the company's initial hypothesis was the fact that more than half its user base came back to the service every single day.

Innovation accounting: Innovation accounting is what makes it possible for startups of all sizes to prove, in an objective way, that they are creating a sustainable business. The process includes three steps, starting with determining the baseline. This involves taking the minimum viable product and doing what you can to determine relevant datapoints that can be referred back to the fact. This could involve things like a pure marketing test to determine if there is actually interest from customers. This, in turn, will make it possible for you to determine a baseline with which to compare the initial cycle of the build, measure, and learn process, too. While better numbers are always desired, poor numbers at this stage aren't terribly important, it only means that the team will have more work to do in the build, measure, and learn cycle.

After the baseline has been determined, the next step is going to be to make the first change to determine what can actually be improved upon. While this certainly makes the entire process take longer than it usually does, making too many changes at once makes it difficult to determine which one of the changes led to the biggest improvement. However, if you have a lot of potential changes to test, you can then test them in groups so when something pops, you will only have to retest a specific range in order to see what caused the inspiration to strike.

Once several build, measure, and learn cycles have been completed, the product should be well on its way from moving from the initial starting point to the final, ideal phase. At some point, however, if things don't seem to be proceeding according to plan, then the question becomes whether it is better to pivot to something new or to stick with the current baseline a while longer to see what improves. The choice between the two should be relatively obvious at this point based on the data provided up to this point.

If the decision is ultimately made to pivot at this point, then it can be quite demoralizing for the team because this means going back to square one, albeit with additional data to draw on in the future. Nevertheless, issues such as vanity metrics or a flawed hypothesis can lead teams down a path that is ultimately not viable. This scenario leaves them no choice but to tear it all down and start again with an alternate hypothesis and a clean slate. It is important to try and reframe the idea of a pivot from a failure to a success because it saved the startup from potentially taking a flawed product to market and paying in a big way further down the line.

There are a few additional types of pivots as well. A Pivot that zooms in is one that takes a signal successful feature of a failed prototype and turns it into its entirely own product. A zoom out pivot, on the other hand, is when a failed prototype is useful enough to become a feature on something larger and more complicated.

The customer segment pivot occurs when the prototype proves solid, but the target audience proves to be different than anticipated. A customer need pivot occurs when it becomes clear that a more pressing problem for the customer exists, so a new product needs to be created to handle it.

A platform pivot occurs when a single application becomes so successful that it spawns an entire related ecosystem. A business architecture pivot occurs when a business switches from having low volume and high margins to high volume and low margins. A value capture pivot is one of the most extreme as it involves restructuring the entire business to generate value in a new way. The engine of growth pivot occurs when the profit structure of the startup changes to keep pace with demand.

Small batches: When given the option to fill a large number of envelopes with newsletters before sending them out, the common approach is to do each step in batches, fold the newsletters, place them in the envelopes, etc. However, this is actually less efficient than doing each piece by itself first, thanks to a concept known as single piece flow, a tenant of Lean manufacturing. In this instance, individual performance is not as important as the overall performance of the system. Time is said to be wasted between each step because things need to be reorganized. If the entire process is looking at a single batch, then efficiency is improved.

Yet another benefit to smaller batches is that it is easier to spot an error in the midst of them. For example, if an error was found in the way the envelopes were folded once all the newsletters had been folded, then that entire step would need to be repeated, adding even more time to the process. On the contrary, a small batch approach would determine this error the first time all the steps were completed.

Andon cord: The Andon Cord was used by Toyota to allow any employee on the production line to halt the entire system if a defect was discovered at any point. While this is a lot of power to give to every team member on the floor, it makes sense as the longer a defect continues through the process, the more difficult and costlier it will eventually take to remove. As such, spotting and calling attention to the problem as quickly as possible is the more efficient choice, even if it means stopping the entire production line until the issue is fixed.

Continuous deployment: Continuous deployment is one of the most difficult Lean Startup processes for many companies to deal with as it means constantly updating live production systems each and every day until they reach an ideal state. The essential lesson is not that everyone should be shipping fifty times per day, but that by reducing batch size you can make it through the entire build, measure, and learn cycle more quickly than your competition can. The ability to learn directly from customers is essential in this scenario as it is one of the primary competitive advantages that startups possess.

Kanban: This is another part of the process that is taken directly from Lean manufacturing. Kanban has four different states. The first of which is the backlog which includes the items that are ready to be worked on but have not yet been actively started on. Next is in progress, which is all of the items that were currently under development. From there, things move to build after development has finished and all the major work has been done so that it is essentially ready for the customer. Finally, the item is validated by a positive review from the customer.

A good rule of thumb is that each of the four stages, also known as buckets, should contain more than three different projects at a time. If a project has been built, for example, it cannot then move into the validation stage until there is room for it. Likewise, work cannot start on items in the backlog until the progress bucket has been cleaned out enough to free up the space. One outcome that many Lean Startups don't anticipate is that this method also makes it easier for teams to measure their productivity based on the validated learning from the customer as opposed to the number of new features being produced.

Five whys: Many technical issues still have a root at a human cause at some point in the process. The five whys technique makes it possible to get close to that root cause from the beginning. It is a deceptively simple plan, but one that is extremely powerful when used by the right hands. The Lean Startup system posits that most problems that are discovered tend to be the result of a lack of personal training, which on the surface can either look like a simple technical issue or even one person's mistake.

For example, with a software company, they may see a negative response from their customers regarding their most recent update. Looking more closely at the issue, it was discovered that this was due to the fact that the update accidentally disabled a popular feature. Looking closer still, this was discovered to be due to a faulty service which failed because a subsystem was used incorrectly due to an engineer that wasn't trained correctly. Looking closer still, you will find that this is due to a fact that a specific manager doesn't believe in giving new engineers the full breadth of training they need because his team is overworked and everybody is needed in one capacity or another.

This type of technique can be especially useful for startups as it gives them the opportunity to determine the true optimum speed needed to make quality improvements. You could invest a huge amount in training, for example, but that doesn't mean this is always going to be the right choice at the given stage of development. However, by looking closely at the root causes of the problems in question, you can more easily determine where there are core areas that require immediate attention as opposed to solely focusing on surface issues.

Another related issue is connected to the fact that many team members are likely prone to overreacting to things at the moment, which is why the 5 Whys are useful when it comes to taking a closer look at what's really happening. There can be a tendency to use the Five Whys to point blame, at first, but the real goal of the Five Whys is to find any chronic problems caused by bad process, not bad people. This is also important to ensure that everyone is in the room together when the analysis takes place because it involves all of the people impacted by the issue, including both customer service and management. If blame has to be taken, it is important that management falls on the sword for not having a team-wide system in place to prevent the issue in the first place.

When it comes to getting started with the Five Whys, the first thing that should be focused on is instilling a feeling of trust and empowerment in the team as a whole. This means being tolerant of all mistakes the first time they happen, while at the same time making it clear that the same mistake should not happen twice. Next, it is important to focus on the system level as most mistakes are made due to a flaw in the system which means it is important to put the focus on this level when it comes to solving problems.

From there, it is important to face the truth, no matter how pleasant or unpleasant it might be. This method may bring up some unpleasantness about the company as a whole but the goal is to fix these issues, after all, and you can't fix what hasn't been brought to light. This is why it is easy to turn it into the Five Blames if you aren't careful which is why the blame should flow up in this instance. Start small and be specific. You want to get the process embedded, so start with small issues with small solutions. Focus on running the process regularly and involving as many people as you can.

Finally, it is important to designate one person on the team as the Five Whys Master. This person will be the one who is primarily in charge of seeing that change actually comes to the team. This, in turn, means they will need a fair amount of authority in order to ensure things get finished. This person will then be the one accountable for any related follow-up, determining if the system is ultimately paying off, or if it is better to cut your losses now and move on. While it can ultimately be a great way to create a more adaptive startup, it can also be harder to get into the groove of than it first appears, so it is important to look at it as a long-term investment rather than something that will be completed in the short-term.

Chapter 2: Create a Useful Lean Startup Experiment

Qualitative or Quantitative: While many people assume that their startup experiment needs to be either quantitative or qualitative, the fact of the matter is that one is not inherently superior to the other. Instead, it is better to think of the two as if one was a hammer and the other was a screwdriver. While a hammer is better at putting nails in wood, that doesn't mean it is inherently superior on all fronts. Any tool can be used for good or evil, which is why it is important to focus more on validating the right metrics than it is to worry about which of these two processes is superior. In fact, using qualitative research and then validating it with quantitative research is likely going to do the most good anyway.

Generative or Evaluative: A generative research technique is one that doesn't start with a hypothesis per se but can still result in a wide variety of different ideas. Things like Customer Discovery Interviews fall under this type of technique. Evaluative, on the other hand, is all about testing a very specific hypothesis in order to determine a very specific result. The popular smoke test falls under this type of testing. It is perhaps this distinction, more than any other, that explains why some people end up with poor results from their experiments.

For example, a smoke test could be run to test the hypothesis that some percentage of the market will be interested in shoes that are compostable. To test this hypothesis, you would then put up a fake coming soon landing page explaining that compostable shoes are totally going to be a thing and see who signs up for the newsletter. After the work was done and the results were in, it turns out that there was about a 1 percent conversion rate when it comes to the shoes. The good news is that the hypothesis was confirmed, the bad news is that it wasn't particularly useful.

What's more, the results are unclear because it still isn't clear if the interest isn't there, if the advertising was poor, or if there is a third variable that you aren't yet aware of. This can be broadly defined as the difference between people not being interested in the value proposition and people not understanding it. The truth of the matter is that there are hundreds of reasons out there why someone might get a false negative result from a given test, just as there are a number of reasons why a false positive might be generated.

To get started, you will need to determine if the hypothesis is flawed or simply vague and, in this case, it is both. Some people are too vague when it comes to a target audience, some are a poor qualifier. As such, first, you would need to focus on a more specific demographic, and second, you would need to do research to determine how big the audience for compostable shoes would ultimately be. Only once the hypothesis is falsifiable and specific can it benefit from an evaluative experiment like the smoke test. If you can't clear up your hypothesis then you will want to start with Generative Research and work back from there.

Market or product: When it comes to the distinction between methods and tools, the biggest is perhaps the distinction between Product and Market. Some methods are useful when it comes to helping startups learn about their customers, their problems, and their best lines of communication. As an example, startups can listen to their potential customers to make it easier for them to understand their specific situations and what their day to day problems are like.

Other methods make it possible to learn about the product or a potential solution that will help to solve a specific problem. One good place to start is with a set of wireframes as a means of determining if the interface is as usable as it seems at face value. Unfortunately, this still won't make it clear if anyone is going to buy anything in the first place.

As these methods don't typically overlap all that well, it is important to choose one and stick with it throughout its cycle. If you combine evaluative research and generative research with Product and Market, you will end up with four different means of determining the best path forward.

Generative Market research asks questions like:

- Who is our customer?
- What are their pains?
- What job needs to be done?
- Is our customer segment too broad?
- How do we find them?

If you can't answer these questions clearly and easily, then your startup is in what is known as the Customer Discovery phase. During this phase, it is important to get to the basis of the problem prior to testing out any potential solutions to ensure that you are actually solving the right problem in the end. If you don't have a clear hypothesis to start, then you will need to generate ideas.

To do so, you may want to talk to customers to see what is bothering them or you could use a data mining approach to determine the problem, assuming you have access to enough data. You may even want to use a survey with open-ended questions if you are really fishing for ideas. Some of these methods will be qualitative and some will be quantitative, but this distinction is ultimately irrelevant in the long run. Data mining is a quantitative approach, but it helps identify problems, most famously the existence of food deserts which would have been difficult to determine in virtually any other way.

Generative Market Research Methods include:

- Surveys
- Focus groups
- Data mining
- Contextual inquiry / ethnography
- Customer Discovery Interviews

Evaluative Market experiment questions include things like:

- How much will they pay?
- How do we convince them to buy?
- How much will it cost to sell?
- Can we use scale marketing?

In order to properly evaluate a specific hypothesis, you may want to start with a landing page to determine if there is likely to be a demand. You may want to put together a basic sales pitch if you are working on a B2B enterprise type product. You could even go so far as to run a conjoint analysis as a means of further understanding the relative positioning of a few value propositions.

Evaluative market experiments that are useful if you have a clear hypothesis include:

- High bar
- Fake door
- Event
- Pocket test
- Flyers
- Pre-sales
- Sales pitch
- Landing page
- Video
- Smoke tests
- Surveys
- Data mining/market research
- Conjoint Analysis
- Comprehension – link to the tool
- 5-second tests

While this sort of research can provide lots of interesting data, it is important to keep in mind that much of it still has the potential to be wrong as signing up for a landing page is very different than actually putting money down on a product. In any situation where the customer doesn't have to commit anything more than an email address, then they don't signify an actual customer demand.

It is important to keep in mind that the value proposition and the product are not the same things. The value proposition is the benefit that your product will deliver to your target audience. As such, you cannot have a validated value proposition if you don't have a validated customer segment.

Chapter 3: Growing a Startup

When a startup is composed of only a few people, the small team that started the company, it's easy to manage everyone and everything. You've got your first few clients, and they're happy with your work, paying all their bills on time and referring your services to other potential clients. But as your startup grows—with more staff, more clients, and more money to keep track of—it can be a challenge to manage all these aspects efficiently.

But there are ways to make this process easier so that you don't lose too much time or money. It's all about ensuring you use collaboration, effective lead generation, and strict budgeting. Here's how:

Collaboration

It doesn't matter if you're working with 5, 25, or 75 employees; any team, regardless of size, needs to have the right tools and resources to successfully collaborate. Teams, whether they are working alongside one another in the same space or remote, need to have awareness of the initiatives their colleagues are pursuing. Yes, there are many collaborative tools available that allow teams to message one another throughout the day and share files, but what these tools often lack is context.

Cage is a new platform that enables contextual collaboration. Through Cage, teams have the ability to gather feedback in real time, assign tasks, edit images, and distribute media files, all on one platform. By facilitating the entirety of a project, from the initial brainstorm to a final review before a video or platform is published, Cage ensures that everyone involved in the projects has full insight into updates and strategic pivots.

Regardless of the medium, every project takes on a life of its own. More often than not, facets shift over time, and these changes and discussions are often implemented across several platforms, which often lead to confusion and oversight. Cage helps teams avoid this pitfall and, as a result, empowers them to collaborate more effectively and efficiently.

Effective lead generation

All startup founders need to focus on revenue efficiency. Otherwise, according to Forbes, you'll be totally lost. Strategic planning and tracking are the only way that you'll be able to ensure you're being as efficient as possible when it comes to revenue and effective lead generation.

LeadCrunch advises that for every dollar spent on customer

acquisition, a company should generate $2.50 in return. But this is not possible if you don't prioritize top-of-the-funnel sales leads. Too many organizations waste time and money by casting large, and irrelevant nets at the top of the funnel, which results in salespeople wasting their time trying to engage customers who, simply, aren't interested. LeadCrunch's CEO, Olin Hyde, believes that the key to successful lead-generation is micro-segmenting, engagement, and nurturing.

Fueled by their AI-driven platform, LeadCrunch allows companies to pinpoint relevant, high-quality prospects, and cultivate deep relationships with them using information that is specific to their unique needs. As a result of their platform's laser-sharp focus, LeadCrunch's top performing customers often see conversion rates spanning 300-1000 percent after leveraging the platform's technology.

Strict budgeting

It's not enough anymore for a startup to use an Excel sheet to calculate and keep track of all their budgeting needs. Even if they've moved onto Google Sheets, which are, after all, free—that's still not enough. If your startup is growing, it makes sense to invest in a B2B budgeting tool that uses actual objective data, which will help you understand how different actions and decisions affect the money coming in.

Hive9, a planning, budgeting, and analytics solution created specifically for B2B marketers, is a smart way for you to keep track of every aspect of budgeting. What's most effective about it? According to Olive & Company, "This comprehensive tool integrates your marketing goals, plan, and budget with your campaigns, so you can measure success and strategically allocate your budget...Hive9 helps you determine where your revenue is coming from, down to a specific touchpoint, and where you can improve your marketing. It also helps determine your cost per marketing lead and sales qualified lead."

According to Hive9's mission, they want to help you create a budgeting plan that you can stick to, one that directly correlates to the complex projects you have going on. They understand how stressful it can be to juggle marketing, which is ever-changing, with budget planning.

Growing your startup is certainly going to be a challenge—but it's a challenge worth taking. After all, change and growth are one of the best ways to ensure your startup thrives and succeeds. By using the strategies of collaboration, effective lead generation, and strict budgeting, you'll be able to improve your startup while also keeping control of all aspects as it grows.

Have you ever grown your startup from its original size? What challenges did you come across, and what strategies did you use to make the transition easier?

Product development

Listen and listen well: Listening is fundamental to a Lean Startup. Listening is what gets you to notice your customers' needs.

It includes listening to devotees and skeptics – your fans will fuel your endeavors and reassure you of all your goodness; skeptics will provide you food for thought on angles perhaps obscured.

Listening will provide you with the "secret to unlock success" and make sense of the noise and valuable feedback that will impact your design iterations, remodeling, and execution.

Educate yourself on laws, regulations, business etiquettes, and many other considerations in your industry.

Your first customers: You must be a die-hard fan of your first customers. After all, they are the ones who were the early adopters, the ones who chose to trust you for the product you introduced to them. And keep selling to them again and again.

Most of the time, startups spend and are more than willing to spend to attract new customers. They forget about their existing customers and do not give importance to re-attracting, reselling, and retaining them.

As a Lean Startup company, your fastest way to feedback for improving your product is the customer who bought it from you at the very start. They tried out your product and knew what was required to make it better for them and many others. Also, your existing happy customers are most likely to spread the word amongst their acquaintances. And referrals are the most authentic and impactful method to increase sales than many other paid programs you are likely to invest in as a startup.

Thus, get feedback from your existing customers and introduce your improved products to them to try out and give you more feedback.

Turn them into loyal customers who will set a precedent of customer value and care for your startup.

Organic outreach: Get to know your customers and let them know you. This is a timeless and evergreen advice for you to grow your Lean Startup faster.

Understand what an SEO audit is and invest in one for your website and social media platforms. An SEO audit will help you create and understand your startup's penetration in the market. Leverage organic outreach and give something of great value to your customers.

A simple combination of great content creation, customer feedback, and input will create a measurable impact on your organic outreach

Content marketing: We are avid fans of content marketing and know that content is here to stay—but only "great" content.

A great content marketing strategy and strategist will make you think of creating resources that are useful to your consumers. Great content will introduce your business properly, talk about its uniqueness, products, and how people think it is doing.

Your social media and website should have sufficient content, updated timely, and posted regularly to keep things fresh and relevant. Therefore, ensure that you create interesting content making use of the many simple tools available in the market.

A strong online presence with an effective SEO strategy and great content will not only help your startup to attract new customers but will also retain existing ones.

Ask your customers to chip in: A great strategy to grow fast is to involve your customers to build a prototype with you.

The lean methodology begins with a true hypothesis – a fairly accurate guesstimate to solve a problem with a product. Introduce the model to your customers and ask them to give you feedback on the usability of the product.

Feedback: Since Lean Startup companies are closely attached to their customers, you will relatively have more convenient time developing content and resources for your customers and prospective audience. Your business model facilitates a fluid and comfortable relationship with your market. And this close relationship can spark a valuable and insightful market research.

Ask your customers for feedback on what they think you are doing regarding selling your products, providing support, quality management, and areas for improvement. Listen carefully and make sure you create a list of their feedback and ideas.

Customer onboarding and satisfaction

As a startup, know your customers personally. Create opportunities to meet them. Many small business brands send handwritten notes with their products to customers to make them feel welcome and part of the family. Send birthday cards, season greetings, etc. to engage your customers.

Share stories of growth, challenges, and outcomes: Your content marketing strategy must include the changes you make, big or small, for example, a new and improved design or a slight color variation, or updating a new phone number to manage queries to the addition of new members in your sales team, etc.

Tell your customers when you make changes to your products based on their feedback, as it will create a circle of trust and reliability which will ultimately affect your bottom line.

Sharing information this way will establish a culture code in your startup and communicate your value proposition via meaningful actions to both your customers and prospective customers.

Accept mistakes: There will be mistakes made on the way. Own them and seek to clarify and apologize appropriately.

Paid outreach

At times, paid marketing and outreach can work brilliantly for a startup. However, you will need to think through before executing this strategy.

The sure sign of a well-paid outreach is profit. You should be making more money with paid outreach per customer than you would in acquiring one. Even if the ratio is 2:1, paid outreach is working.

By the end of the day, your goal is to make customers happy. When your customers are happy with your product, they will refer you to their friends and family, and you will continue to succeed in your endeavors.

And this leads us to our suggestion of looking into influencer marketing. Influencer marketing will involve your happy customers to become your brand ambassadors and talk about your product in their social circles to co-build your brand.

It is a win-win for you, your existing customers, and your potential customers who will have been influenced by their friends or influencers. This way, your startup's value proposition travels smoothly into the market.

Build a great team

Keep good people around you. Keep people who know what they are doing. Keep people who thrive on feedback and know how to use that feedback for growth and improvement; this is key to the interactive model of improving your product and keeping it relevant to your customers' needs.

Learn from examples: These are some examples of well-known companies who did not want to waste their time, their customers' time, or that of their investors. They got down to developing the product that would fulfill the needs of their customers.

When Dropbox came across the lean methodology, the company began thinking about their product which at the time of its inception was competing with many other similar products.

They learned how to test new products with their customers and incorporated their feedback. From 100,000 registered users, Dropbox went over 4,000,000 in only 15 months with the Lean Startup principles.

The giant General Eclectic also went into the Lean methodology to develop faster solutions with FastWorks - a complete mindset changing program to how things usually worked at GE. A very popular example was the development of a gas turbine two years faster with 40% less cost. The lean methodology is not only for startups after all!

After approaching local shoe stores and grabbing photos of their shoes with consent, the owner of Zappos tested his hypothesis of whether an online shoe-selling site would work.

And it did! Zappos is the largest online shoe store with over 1000 brands featured.

The ideas above are fairly consistent with the ideas you hear every day. You learned these at business schools, through books and blogs, and friends and colleagues. Simple as they may sound, it is always the simpler ideas that are key to great outcomes.

Chapter 4: Six Sigma Basics

Six Sigma is the name of a lean system for measuring quality with the ultimate goal of getting as close to perfection as feasibly possible. Ideally, a company that is running at Six Sigma maximum efficiency would generate, at most only 3.4 defects per million attempts at a particular process. Zshift is the name given to these deviations which show the difference between a poorly completed process and a perfectly completed one. The baseline Zshift is 4.5 while the ideal value is 6. Processes that have not yet been analyzed via the Six Sigma process typically score somewhere between 1 and 2.

Levels of Zshift: If the Six Sigma analysis of a process is at 1, then this means you can expect customers to get exactly what they want somewhere around 30 percent of the time. If this is increased to a Zshift 2, then you can expect the process to give the customers exactly what they are looking for about 70 percent of the time. If the process reaches a 3, then it will be accurate about 93 percent of the time, a 4 will be 99 percent accurate, and a 5 and 6 reach even smaller divisions towards the goal of 100 percent accuracy and customer satisfaction.

Six Sigma cert: Within Six Sigma, there are a variety of different certification levels that can be achieved, each with its own tasks and responsibilities as it relates to the whole. Six Sigma is all about decreasing the risk of production errors by reducing waste and improving efficiency. The first two levels of certification, White and Yellow Belts, are crucial to this part of the process as, while working under higher level Sigmas, they do things like ensure the data that is coming in is on the right track and carry out specific functions that are designed to add overall value to the process. These certificates are also a great way to be exposed to the overall Six Sigma methodology.

The next level of certification is the Green Belt which allows holders to work more directly on Six Sigma projects being helped by those above them while also allowing them to oversee projects being handled by Yellow and White Belts. Black Belts then lead high-level projects while also supporting and monitoring those at other tiers. Finally, Master Black Belts are those who are often brought in specifically to start Six Sigma at a company and are knowledgeable to mentor everyone at every level.

Six Sigma is the tool for you if...

While almost any company and any team can benefit from the Six Sigma in some shape or form, this doesn't mean it is always going to be the right choice, especially for a startup company. In fact, deciding if it is the right choice or not actually depend on a wide variety of different specifics, including how committed the team is to implementing the system in the first place and what the company's developing culture is like.

Leadership involvement is key: When discussing the idea of transitioning to Six Sigma, it is important to not look at it as another type of flash in the pan management style that is going to go out of fashion as quickly as it appeared. Instead, it is far more likely to find purchase if it is pitched as an enhancement of an existing system. Likewise, you can always find opposition to something new from someone in the company which is why it is important to start with buy-in from the top and work your way down the list from there. It is extremely important to have the full management team on board from the start as if it doesn't look like there is a consensus regarding the new system, then it is going to be dead in the water before it even gets off the ground.

This doesn't mean that the entire team needs to be committed to the idea of Six Sigma from the start, but it does mean that it is vital that the change that is on the horizon that needs to be institutional which means the leadership needs to put forth a united front. Don't forget, the human brain is a creature of habit which means that it will recoil from new systems that seem too complicated if the system is, at all, perceived as optional. As such, if there is an opposition to the new system, stress the idea that it is important it be expressed in private.

Consider the infrastructure: Six Sigma is all about leaders mentoring those on their teams in order to make Six Sigma work as effectively as possible. As such, if you hope to transition to a Six Sigma system successfully, then this needs to be a full-time job for at least one person, at least until the new, positive, habits have formed for good. While this might not seem cost-effective in the short-term the Six Sigma savings that will appear once the system is up and running properly are sure to more than make up for it.

Consider what will boost compliance: After support of management has been assured and the infrastructure is in place to make the project really pop, the next step will be to ensure that the rest of the team members have a motivational reason to fall in line. While active rewards aren't going to be required once the Six Sigma process has been properly internalized, they are a good way to help the team get used to looking at problems as though Six Sigma is the solution. While the right way to track team progress is going to be different for every team, it is vital that each member of the team feels an immediate and compelling reason to commit to the new program, at least at first.

After all, companies are like any other body that is currently in motion, the bigger the company, the more inertia is needed when making large changes. This is where your startup has the opportunity to outmaneuver the big boys and start gaining some ground as quickly as possible.

Who else is using Six Sigma in your field: While Six Sigma has proven its worth in a wide variety of different fields, this doesn't mean that each of these fields is going to be ready to adopt the process with open arms immediately. While looking to the future is one thing, if your startup is also going to the first company to adopt Six Sigma as a common practice in its industry, then you need to be prepared from extreme resistance from every side and especially any members of the old guard that you may have brought on to ensure the real work gets done. Luckily, the science behind Six Sigma is solid which is why it should be fairly easy to come up with specific examples of how it can help your company to silence any opposition.

Consider training objectives: Depending on the size of your team, training everyone as a whole might make sense. Eventually, however, different training levels are going to need to be enforced, as not everyone is going to need to be a Black Belt. As such, it is important to look more closely at the various levels and the qualifications for each before determining how training can best be broken up for maximum effectiveness. It is important to also factor in how the training will affect any other duties the trainees might have as well as what areas are going to be focused on most stringently.

Taking the time to work out the specifics of your training scenario before you get started is sure to make all the difference in the world when it comes to implementing Six Sigma successfully. Remember, there are no one-size-fits-all options in this scenario which means planning out the specifics of your team's training could literally be the success and failure of the entire project. What's more, it can also make other issues more apparent when otherwise, they would not have been noticed until training was already underway.

Consider flagship projects: After the Six Sigma training is out of the way, it is important to have a few important projects waiting in the wings in order to show the team that the system is worth it. Not only will these projects help to get the entire team excited about Six Sigma, but they will also be useful down the line if questions as to whether or not Six Sigma is worth keeping start popping up as well. As a general rule, you will want to start with at least a Green or Black belt project and then do everything in your power in order to ensure they end up being successful.

While doing so, it is also important to not spread the Black

Belts and Green Belts that you have on your team too thin that it makes them struggle to match their deliverables. Instead, it is better to have too many people on a few projects to ensure they are completed to perfection. Remember, if things go according to plan then you will have plenty of time to complete other projects once these go over like gangbusters.

Furthermore, it is important that these early chapters are more than just fluff projects, they need to be things that are legitimately beneficial to the company as a whole. If your early projects are heavily publicized but do little to produce viable results, then you run the risk of Six Sigma being seen as little more than a fad with lots of flash and little substance. You can ensure that this doesn't happen by instead choosing projects that have a clear value, regardless of whether the person making the decisions is trained in Six Sigma or not. Remember, public opinion is one of the most important resources to covet at this stage and will continue to be so until Six Sigma has become a habit for the entire team.

Chapter 5: Implementing Six Sigma

Give the team a reason to want to try Six Sigma: In order to ensure that Six Sigma is implemented successfully, it is vital that you take the time to motivate your team in the most effective way possible, so they understand why it is so important to adopt the Six Sigma methodology. Depending on the state your startup company is in, the burning platform scenario might be the best choice.

The burning platform is a type of motivational technique whereby you explain that the situation your company finds itself in is just as perilous as standing on a burning platform and the only way to turn things around for good is by implementing Six Sigma. It is important to have stats that back this idea up, though fudging the numbers for productivities sake might not hurt either. Adapting to Six Sigma can be difficult for team members who are set in their ways and external motivation may be just what the doctor ordered.

Give team members the tools they need: After the primary round of Six Sigma training has finished, it will be important to ensure that you have a strong mentorship program in place, along with details on the finer points of the process for those who need them. One of the worst things that can happen at this point is for a team member to express an interest in the program only to become disinterested when additional materials are not readily available. A team member who cannot easily find answers to their questions is a team member who will not follow Six Sigma processes when it really counts.

Prioritize properly: Regardless of the situation, there are always going to be a variety of potential outcomes. While talking and planning for Six Sigma is one thing, taking steps to actively prioritize it is another entirely. When team members see those in leadership roles prioritize Six Sigma outcomes, it makes them more likely to prioritize Six Sigma activities in their own jobs as well. Additionally, it is important to make it clear that quality is critical, as is listening to the customer when it comes to ensuring Six Sigma leads to measurable results so that team members of all level of certification can keep an eye on the overall progress the company is making.

Make it a group thing: When it comes to tutoring your team about Six Sigma, it is important to ensure that they make personal connections with how it will affect their jobs for the better so that they feel more personally invested in the program's overall success. This may come about by ensuring the entire team is able to provide buy-in or making different team members responsible for enforcing different aspects of the Six Sigma process as taking the time to ensure that everyone feels connected to seeing Six Sigma succeed will ensure personal retention rates remain as high as possible.

Track the results: Determining a realistic metric that can determine appropriate levels of success before and after Six Sigma is an important step in the process as it can provide you with the motivating data that is required to ensure that Six Sigma adoption is at an all-time high. On the other hand, if it turns out that the system actually ends up being ineffective, then you will be the first to know as well. Regardless, having a viable metric to properly determine aptitude is sure to come in handy more than once. What's more, assuming the results are positive then it is sure to be a great motivating factor for the entire team and provide yet another reason why sticking with Six Sigma is so important.

Reward team players: While offering viable reasons for the team to adopt Six Sigma is one thing, it is still important to provide positive reinforcement during the early days so that everyone is constantly motivated to follow the Six Sigma process until it becomes a habit. The goal here should be to choose a reward that is valuable while at the same time not being so extravagant that eventually removing it won't completely remove the team's desire to keep up the good work.

Six Sigma criticism

Six Sigma is just a fad: While it has only been back in the spotlight for a few years, the fact of the matter is that the origins of Six Sigma can be traced all the way back to the early 1900s when it was used by entrepreneurs like Henry Ford, Edward Deming, and Walter Shewhart. Additionally, it further separates itself from true fad management styles by being more focused on the use of data as a means of ensuring the best decision is made at the moment as possible, specifically those with a focus on the customer as a means of ensuring a viable return on every investment.

Switching to Six Sigma is resource intensive: While it's true that training the team in the Six Sigma process is time-consuming, the end goal is for it to save far more time than the training will cost in the long run by ensuring team members do their jobs as effectively as possible moving forward.

It is important to remember the story of the pair of lumberjacks who worked day after day in the forest. One man worked himself to the point of exhaustion every day while the other man spent the time preparing properly, and at the end of the day, both men had always chopped the same amount of wood. If your team has the opportunity to work smarter instead of harder, why wouldn't you provide them with the tools they need to make that the new norm.

Furthermore, the cost of training the team the Six Sigma process can be further mitigated over time by spreading out the training courses as required. While this means the team won't start seeing the results as quickly as might otherwise be the case, even getting the entire team up to Yellow Belt will produce noticeable results. Furthermore, any funds put towards this type of training can really be seen as an investment in the business as a whole and should be treated accordingly.

Our team is too small for Six Sigma to be effective: While the effectiveness of Six Sigma is proportionate to the inefficiency of the processes previously in place, that doesn't mean it doesn't have something to offer companies that are just getting up and running as well. After all, Six Sigma offers a different way of looking at the types of business interactions that happen day to day in hopes of increasing productivity and, as a result, profits as well, regardless of the size of the team that is utilizing it. What's more, smaller teams will actually be able to take on the Six Sigma mantle more easily than larger companies as the number of resources required to train 10 team members are always going to be far lower than what it would cost to train 50 instead.

Furthermore, smaller businesses can be hindered more by production bottlenecks which means a Six Sigma system would potentially be able to lead to greater periods of growth as issues that may not otherwise have been addressed for years are taken care of before they become institutional problems. Regardless of the size of the company in question, taking the time to truly streamline relevant processes or improve customer relations is always going to be the right choice.

Six Sigma doesn't apply here: While it's true that Six Sigma isn't going to apply to every single industry across the board, it has moved beyond its manufacturing sector roots. Furthermore, studies show that industries that provide services are prone to more waste than the manufacturing sector in the first place. This is due to the fact that so much of what is produced is intangible that it makes standardizing any process extremely difficult. This is where Six Sigma comes in as it has plenty of processes in place to track the services that are being provided which can ultimately be used to improve efficiency.

Six Sigma is difficult to use practically: While it may have a reputation for being all about the numbers, a vast majority of the tools and principles that are used in implementing Six Sigma require less math and more common sense. As an example, consider the mitigation of waste which is one of the most important aspects of Six Sigma, and something that only requires an understanding of the business in question and how it can be done in a more effective fashion. This is indicative of most of Six Sigma which is largely about fostering the mentality that makes it possible for team members to find the root cause of an issue, regardless of how long it might take. While formulas and mathematical equations may be used, they are simply a justification for this fact.

Lean is plenty for now: When expressing the benefits of Six Sigma, it is important to make it clear that it is a variation of the Lean system, not a replacement for it. In fact, the system is often referred to as Lean Six Sigma. When used in conjunction with one another, Lean will then the throughput and speed of the process and simplifying to ensure that the team is able to do the best with what they have available. Six Sigma then takes these improved processes and makes them of the highest quality possible by reducing defects and, as a result, lowers the deviation. Combining the two can only lead to better results overall.

Chapter 6: Additional Strategies

Kaizen

The word Kaizen translates to "continuous improvement" which is obviously an important goal when it comes to creating the most effective Lean system possible. The goal of the Kaizen strategy is to ensure that all of the talent within the team is always focusing on improving whenever and wherever possible. This strategy is relatively unique for a Lean strategy in that it is more than just a direct plan of action, it is also a general philosophy for the company as a whole. The goal of Kaizen is to create a culture that is supportive of improvement in all of its forms while also creating groups that are focused directly on improving key processes and reaching well-defined goals.

Kaizen is a great strategy to implement while you are standardizing your work process as the two complement one another well. Standard practices lead to current best practices which Kaizen can then improve upon. The Kaizen strategy can be useful when it comes to improving any strategy that your team uses with any real degree of regularity as long as you are fully aware of the end goal for the updated process. From there, you will need to review the current state of things before adding any improvements. From there it is just a matter of following up properly in order to ensure any proffered improvements work as expected.

Training the team in Kaizen actually serves double duty as it teaches them to apply the philosophy and the plan of action at the same time. This type of thinking is often habitually formed by those who are constantly looking for ways to improve their most commonly used processes while also allowing other team members to approach common tasks in new and innovative ways as required. This mindset should naturally be nurtured whenever possible as it is the only way to ensure more fruitful results in the long run.

While constantly improving existing practices is a great place to start, it is important that the Kaizen your team is practicing does not only occur after the fact. When new processes are created, it is best for everyone that they are held to the same examination process as any other. Hindsight is useful, foresight gets results.

Kaizen steps
- The first thing you will need to do is to standardize your process, not just the process that you are looking to put through the Kaizen process but all the processes to ensure that any eventual improvements are as beneficial as possible.

- Next, you will need to compare the processes at play in order to determine where steps that are being used in some processes can be used successfully elsewhere as well. When taking this step, it is vital that you look at true KPIs as opposed to anecdotal information for this step as, otherwise, it can be easy to get off on wrong track without even realizing it.

- After you have determined where real change should occur, the next step is to consider what you currently have available to make completing the process as easy as possible. During this period, you will want to consider the start of the project as well as its conclusion and then brainstorm all the possible ways to reach point B from point A. While no idea should be off the table at first, it is important that you ensure you only move forward with ideas that are truly useful as well as innovative as innovation for innovation's sake is only going to create waste.

- The final step is going to be to repeat as needed so that new innovations become standard operating procedures so that you can then begin the entire process anew. When it comes to Kaizen, the only bad idea is to rest on your laurels.

Creating a Kaizen mindset: Getting the entire team together for a Kaizen event where everyone brainstorms ways to streamline a specific process is relatively straightforward. However, training your team to always work from a Kaizen mindset can be a far more difficult task. Difficult does not mean impossible, however, and the best way to start to train them to this improved way of thinking is to focus on creating a corporate culture where elimination of waste is everyone's top priority. If you can keep this idea in the team's mindset, during every meeting, every performance review, every informal conversation, day in and day out, then eventually team members will start noticing waste without even having to consciously think about it. Once this occurs they will be well on their way to finding ways to work around it instead.

With this done, you will also want to start to set aside a specific time each day to allow team members to look at the processes they use every single day and do nothing else but really think hard about them. It is important to always remember that the human mind loves repetition almost as much as it loves patterns which is why it is so easy to follow the steps for a process you have done a hundred times without even thinking about it. While this can make the process go faster if the steps involved are optimized, it can also make it easy to complete the process with blinders on and not notice points of inefficiency while you are in the midst of them. As such, providing the team with the time they need to think about their processes separate from actually doing them will let them look at the entire project from a different angle.

If you take this exercise a step further, you will then provide the team with an opportunity to talk to the rest of the team about their processes as well. This cross-pollination of ideas will give each process an entirely fresh set of eyes which will provide insight into even more blind spots. This is especially useful for particularly complex processes, just make sure that everyone takes detailed notes, so nothing gets lost in the shuffle. Additionally, it is important to emphasize that there are no wrong answers during this stage, a free and open dialogue can provide solutions to problems that you previously weren't even aware you were facing.

Poka-Yoke

The Lean system strategy known as Poka-Yoke is most accurately translated as actively guarding against mistakes. Essentially, Poka-Yoke can be thought of as a variety of failsafe procedures that are naturally built into any processes specifically for the purpose of catching common errors. Poka-yoke is best used on tasks that are especially repetitive, require precise repetition across numerous steps, or require an extreme period of focus to use correctly. This tool is an especially beneficial type of Muda that works to ensure the overall value while not necessarily creating any of its own.

When Poka-Yoke is at its most effective, it relies on a thorough understanding of the steps in every process as well as additional ways of mitigating potential pain points as effectively and cheaply as possible, while also taking care not to create any new bottlenecks as a result.

Control Poka-Yoke: Control Poka-Yoke does not allow the next step of the process to move forward until a found error has been corrected. As an example, the way a USB dongle is designed so that you cannot plug it in unless it is facing the right way is a Control Poka-Yoke as it ensures you cannot plug in the device in such a way that it will not work once you do so.

Warning Poka-Yoke: Warning Poka-Yoke, as the name implies, provides the team member completing the process that they made an error on a proceeding step.

Contact method Poke-Yoke: The contact method Poka-Yoke works under an assumption that a third party, either a device or a person, is monitoring the steps that are being taken to ensure no errors materialize. A spell-check program is a good example of this type of Poka-Yoke. Contact method Poka-Yoke is especially useful if the same task needs to be repeated as quickly as possible in order for the process to run smoothly.

In order to determine where Poka-Yoke can be of the most use to your processes, the first thing you will need to do is to determine which steps in the process already cause the most harm, or have the most potential to cause harm, in the shortest period of time overall. You may want to start by determining the processes' critical features and then looking at potential causes of failure before determining a signal method that will work effectively in the situation.

Fixed Value Poka-Yoke: This type of Poka-Yoke is useful in situations where the overall process is quite short but requires the same step in the process to be run numerous times in a row. Poka-Yoke is useful in scenarios like this as they allow the person who is completing the process to know how many times they have repeated a specific step. As an example, think of an administrative assistant making numerous copies of a document who first counts out the amount of paper they need to ensure they don't have to count each as it is made.

Motion step Poka-Yoke: This type of Poka-Yoke is useful in situations where a team member needs to perform numerous different tasks, in a specific order, many times. This Poka-Yoke determines when specific steps have been completed to ensure the team member completing the process remains on track. As an example, consider any website where you are asked to enter your payment information. When the website tells you that you haven't entered the correct payment details and can also track that you haven't yet checked the box to prove you aren't a robot, then it is an example of motion step Poka-Yoke.

Self-Check Poka-Yoke: This type of Poka-Yoke requires the fewest additional resources to complete and instead just requires a little extra time to give the team member performing the process the opportunity to check their work before they move on to each new step. This is a good choice for scenarios where mistakes are extremely obvious, and its biggest drawback is that it requires extra time during which the team member must remain focused as well.

Task Poka-Yoke: This type of Poka-Yoke is useful when it comes to processes that require a team member to directly come into contact with a customer as it helps cut down on mistakes that are made in live situations. A great example of this is the change machines at grocery stores that prevent cashiers from making mistakes when counting out change.

Treatment Poka-Yoke: This type of Poka-Yoke works to ensure that the customer always has a positive and efficient interaction whenever they encounter a team member while working through the course of a specific process. The goal here is to standardize what team members say as much as possible in an effort to prevent any potential mistakes before they happen. This is especially useful for new businesses as it gives new team members something to fall back on when they encounter something new, which is basically everything at this point. A great example of this type of Poka-Yoke is the scripts call centers use.

Tangible Poka-Yoke: This type of Poka-Yoke aims to standardize the physical element of the customer's experience. In situations where individual customers have widely varying needs, this type of Poka-Yoke is often the best way to standardize service. A good example of this type of Poka-Yoke is uniforms.

Preparation Poka-Yoke: This type of Poka-Yoke: aims to work with the customer directly to influence expectations and goals prior to the experience. Depending on the requirements surrounding the products or service in your business, this can be a great way to make sure that customers are prepared properly before they speak to a team member to ensure the whole process goes as smoothly as possible. A good example of this type of Poka-Yoke are menus that are visible to patrons of fast food restaurants before they order so the actual order process proceeds as smoothly as possible.

Conclusion

Thank you for making it through to the end of *Lean Startup: The Complete Step-by-Step Lean Six Sigma Startup Guide*, let's hope it was informative and able to provide you with all of the tools you need to achieve your goals. Just because you've finished this book doesn't mean there is nothing left to learn on the topic; expanding your horizons is the only way to find the mastery you seek. Additionally, it is important to keep in mind that, while there is some overlap between any two startups, much of what is going to take place is going to be largely unique to the startup in question.

After all, isn't the point of a startup to do something new? As such, it is important to understand that while following the Lean Startup strategy can certainly lead to success, sometimes you may have to make your own way because what you are trying to do is so out there that the existing methods of testing don't apply. This doesn't mean that you should abandon all that the Lean way of doing things has done for you thus far, it simply means that you will need to take what you have learned and use that to create logical ways to test whatever it is you are prototyping. Likewise, it is important to not get impatient and try to rush the process. After all, creating a viable product or service that a targeted portion of the audience is interested in is a marathon and not a sprint which means the slow and steady wins the race.

Finally, if you found this book useful in any way, a review on Amazon is always appreciated!

www.ingramcontent.com/pod-product-compliance
Lightning Source LLC
Chambersburg PA
CBHW070957240526
45469CB00016B/1476